Cuba for Christ!

The Amazing Revival

Open Doors

Sovereign World

Scripture quotations are taken from
The Holy Bible, New International Version.
© 1973, 1978, 1984 International BIble Society.
Used by permission.

ISBN: 1 85240 250 4

SOVEREIGN WORLD LIMITED
P.O. Box 777, Tonbridge, Kent TN11 0ZS, England.

Typeset and printed in the UK by Sussex Litho Ltd, Chichester, West Sussex.

Foreword

'Cuba Para Cristo!' Cuba for Christ! I wish the Christians of every country would adopt this prayer slogan for their own land. And I wish that the accompanying revival Cuba has experienced would be our experience too.

But perhaps we ought to be careful about what we wish for others. Because revival doesn't come without a cost. In this booklet, you will read about the price that Cuban Christian leaders paid before the revival – on their knees – and as a result of the revival – most often in prison.

On one of my early trips to the island, a young Cuban doctor took me to a hospital in Havana. A quotation from their revolutionary hero and 'martyr', Che Guevara, was chiselled on the wall and caught my eye: "If this revolution is not aimed at changing people, then I am not interested."

The fruit of revival in Cuba is indeed changed lives. Cuba watchers estimate that at least one million lives have been changed in the past eight years. That is ten per cent of the total population! A significant house church movement has developed across the entire island as a result. And a shortage of Bible study books continues to exist to this day.

The impact of these changed lives has been felt at the highest levels. So much so that Fidel Castro has reportedly been meeting with evangelical Church leaders. They have been discussing family values and how to instill Christian ethics and morality into the young people on the island.

My early preaching trips to Cuba were to encourage the believers and to prepare them for the coming impact of the Marxist revolution. I used lessons we had learned from the Church in Eastern Europe and the Soviet Union. What Cuba needs today are those who can share with her leaders how to prepare for the coming era of freedom. Again, the chaos which openness brought to Eastern Europe and the former Soviet Union is a model to avoid. May God raise up these teachers from amongst you who read this booklet.

I will never forget the words of a dear Cuban pastor on one of my last trips to Cuba, "Thank you Brother Andrew, for not forgetting us!" His voice shook with emotion. "Tell the people in the West that we also have not forgotten them. We pray for them every day that materialism will not water down their faith."

Brother Andrew

Revival prayers

The young Cuban pastor made his way to the front of the meeting. His heart was pounding. But he knew that God had given him something very important to say. It was September 1986. The occasion, an Open Doors meeting in Toronto, Canada. As the Cuban came to the platform, his quiet conviction prompted the organisers to give him the microphone without any questions.

The man quietly introduced himself to the audience as Pastor Eusebio from Cuba. He was embarrassed by his limited English. But he so wanted to speak, that he plunged straight into his message.

"Brother Andrew, when you first came to Cuba, I was there. But I was being held in prison. I heard from my pastor friends what an encouragement your visits were. A few years later, you sent two Dutch ladies to Cuba. The Holy Spirit guided them to meet me in Lenin Park and there they gave me Bibles and gifts for our church. The encouragement from that one encounter gave me the strength to persevere for six months!

Finally, I was facing so much pressure, I had to leave Cuba, but I have promised to pray and do everything I can to help my brothers and sisters in Christ on the island. Each one of you here can go as a tourist and have a big impact by encouraging our growing Christian family in Cuba. I can give you the names of pastors and people you could visit."

Brother Andrew strongly challenged the people attending the meeting to be involved and go. And Pastor Eusebio added, "You must first visit my good friend, Pastor Manuel, when you go to Cuba!"

Pastor Manuel was agonising in prayer and fasting in the sanctuary of his little church building – so similar to the many other humble house churches tucked away in the valleys and rolling mountains of Cuba. It was Tuesday of Holy Week, 1987. With the Good Friday and Easter services soon approaching, he was desperate to see a breakthrough over the spiritual stronghold that gripped his island homeland.

His mind reviewed the pressures under which he had served the Lord for the past 25 years. His normal enthusiasm was flagging. He understood better than ever how Jesus must have felt during those days just before his crucifixion.

Again he cried out in agony, "Oh, Lord. We have so many needs here in Cuba. Who can help us?"

After what seemed like many hours, God's still small voice responded, "Brother Eusebio in Canada."

"But Lord," Pastor Manuel countered, "how can I contact my friend, Pastor Eusebio? My post is monitored, the phones are bugged. I'm completely cut off!"

At that precise moment, Pastor Manuel heard knocking on the door of his little house attached to the church. He got up from his knees, walked over and opened the door and was amazed to see two visitors carrying large bags. One spoke in Spanish, "Greetings from Pastor Eusebio in Toronto." The two visitors were astonished to see the tears flowing down Pastor Manuel's face.

They shared the presents they had brought; Bibles, food and gifts. The fellowship in that little ramshackle house for the next hour was to them a foretaste of heaven. Then another hour rushed by as Pastor Manuel shared his vision for revival and evangelism in Cuba.

This visit prompted the tall, softly-spoken pastor to put his vision into writing. It was a passionate appeal. A few months later, it was spread around the world. It reads as follows:

Please join us in prayer

I have been serving the Lord for more than 25 years under difficult circumstances, which only the one who has experienced them could understand. For many years, we have been praying and shedding many tears for the work of

God here in Cuba. God has promised us a great revival and we are sure that the hour of God is coming for us. Praise the Lord!

The Lord has given me some verses for this very hour and one of them is: *"Can plunder be taken from warriors, or captives rescued from the fierce? But this is what the Lord says: 'Yes, captives will be taken from warriors, and plunder retrieved from the fierce; I will contend with those who contend with you, and your children I will save.'"* (Isaiah 49:24-25)

I beg you in the love of God, as we read in Ezekiel 22:30, that you stand in the gap with us, building up a wall of salvation. Do you think the Lord will find in you somebody ready to intercede for a Christian people? I ask you to pray and make contact with other pastors, leaders and prayer teams. You can make a copy of this letter and send it to others inside and outside your country.

Join us on 1st November 1987 in a prayer and fasting crusade for Cuba and hope you will see the answer of deliverence from God. Amen.

This letter prompted thousands of Christians all over the world to begin praying and fasting for a revival in Cuba.

Elsewhere in Cuba, another dedicated pastor, Juan, was also agonising in prayer and fasting in the sanctuary of his little church building. It was a Tuesday morning in 1987. His heart was pounding as he begged God to bring revival to his country. He had spent the past year criss-crossing the countryside, seeking out both rural and urban church leaders who shared his vision for God to pour out revival on the Church in Cuba.

As he prayed that day, a picture came into Pastor Juan's mind. He saw a map of the whole island of Cuba with a cross passing over it and slowly changing it. Then the words flashed across the image: 'Cuba Para Cristo' (Cuba for Christ). He was so excited by this vision, he rushed to share it with his friends. Soon a regular daily prayer meeting was being held in his own church, asking God to bring revival. This developed into a round the clock, seven days a week prayer chain, with different teams praying every half hour. In addition, two days a week were set aside for corporate prayer and fasting.

Pastor Juan's travels across the island fanned into flames the spreading vision to believe God that all Cuba could be won for Christ. Regular prayer meetings became part of life in many areas of the country. And before the end of 1988, a nationwide 24-hour-a-day-prayer chain had been formed, that continued every day and night for one year – passionate people pleading with God for an outpouring of his Holy Spirit. Leaders and church members alike became well known for their calloused knees. The 100,000 Christians across the land of ten million people were caught up with the slogan, 'Cuba Para Cristo'. God heard. And God answered!

Revival
fires

Prayer is a powerful spiritual weapon. And the united prayer of brothers and sisters across the entire island of Cuba moved the heart of God. Soon reports came that this prayer movement had crossed all denominational barriers. Visitors to the island would return and share with tears their joy at seeing pastors and leaders of various denominations on their knees praying together in the early morning.

The first report of the special outpouring of God's Spirit came in 1988, from a small town south-east of Havana. The pastor and congregation had been praying and fasting for revival. Later, the pastor reported that as people entered the little church, they would begin to cry. People began lining up at two in the morning to get into the prayer meetings. So the pastor decided to invite a retired evangelist to come and preach as they continued to fast and pray.

One night, a lame man was brought to the service and the Lord healed him instantly. Other miracles occurred. Word spread immediately and widely. Before long, large crowds arrived at the meetings in the small church. Sometimes busloads of people from other cities came. One weekend, they reported over 8,000 visitors (to a church that could seat less than 300). They would hold as many as 20 services a day. Many Sundays, the pastor, his assistant and two of the young people counselled over 300 people wanting to become Christians. Often the streets around the church were blocked due to the enormous crowds attending the services. They would squeeze 400 into the small building and put 400 on the roof.

Within the space of six months, over 100,000 people passed through the doors of this little church in Madruga. It was impossible to accurately record how many people had become

Christians during this time.

A community to the west of Havana invited an evangelist to come and preach. The young daughter of a civic official there was confined to a wheelchair after a number of operations. When the evangelist prayed over her at one of the meetings, she was immediately healed and walked away – pushing the wheelchair! She was followed down the street by a large crowd, praising God. Many turned to the Lord in this city as a result of that miracle.

One of the reoccuring miracles that happened during the revival was the healing of teeth! This included, unbelievably, the filling, straightening and whitening of teeth. One pastor explained that he thought these mysterious fillings were how God was glorified. A tooth restored to its natural state could be claimed to be good in the first place. But tooth filling materials such as silver were not available to Cuban dentists – so only God could have miraculously filled the teeth.

In the east end of the island, one particular dentist wanted to publicly ridicule his family who were believers. He said he would prove that the accounts of teeth being healed were lies. He attended a church service with his family – and during the service he began to cry out because God suddenly healed and repaired his own teeth! Not surprisingly, he became a Christian that night.

But even as the wind of revival was sweeping the country, opposition to this move of God began to grow too. On 13th February 1989, the two pastors of this church were imprisoned, along with 11 other church members, including two 65-year-old men. The newly-painted church facade was defaced with graffiti proclaiming the glory of the Communist Party. One read, 'We believe neither in miracles nor healing.'

A town in central Cuba was the scene of an amazing event in this revival that swept across the entire island. In January 1991, an evangelist was invited to the small Pentecostal church in town to preach at a week of special meetings.

Two paralysed people were brought to the meeting in wheelchairs and placed at the front. One was an older person, and one was a young person who had been crippled from birth. The evangelist was preaching about Jesus healing a paralytic and he said, "It was just like my saying to these two people, 'Stand up and walk!'"

The younger paralytic immediately stood up out of his wheelchair and said to the older one, "He said, stand up and walk!"

The older replied, "But I can't. I'm crippled!"

The younger one countered, "Here, let me help you." Soon both were on their feet excitedly walking around the room and praising God.

The news spread like wildfire and the church became overcrowded. In no time at all, the pastor was holding a number of services daily. As soon as one service ended, the church building was cleared so that the next meeting could begin. The church leaders were exhausted.

The crowds outside the church were so large that they blocked the traffic in the streets. It wasn't long before the police began complaining about this. The pastor requested the use of the community sports stadium for the meetings to avoid the problem. The police returned with a negative response to his request, but suggested that they divert the traffic away from the church. They then allowed the pastor and evangelist to bring their PA system to the door of the church building and preach to the crowds in the street! This was the first known legal outdoor public preaching in Cuba under the Castro regime.

That weekend, over 23,000 people heard the Gospel and thousands responded to the call of Christ. Today this church is overflowing and many new house churches have been established in the area to disciple the new believers.

Results

By 1991, conservative estimates suggest that the Church in Cuba had grown to over one million believers strong. Significant church growth was recorded all over the island.

The first result of the revival was that the prevalent myth under Castro's regime – 'There is no God' – was destroyed. Today, the Cuban Church is full of young people who grew up under the teachings of an atheistic system. Even official Party members are showing an interest in the Gospel.

Secondly, the miracles which God performed crossed all denominational boundaries. These signs and wonders occurred in Baptist and Methodist circles as well as Pentecostal. The once defensive mood and attitude in the Cuban Church was turned into an offensive one. The cry all over the island continues today: 'Cuba Para Cristo'!

The Church grew so significantly that a new network of house churches sprang up. By the end of 1991, the revival had generated more than 2,400 house churches. By the mid-90s, they outnumbered official churches three to one. Today, estimates place the number of house churches at well over 10,000 and the other evangelical churches at approximately 1,200.

The cost of revival

In the earlier and darker days of Fidel Castro's regime, Cubans were often afraid to even go into a church building. One couple who were schoolteachers lost their jobs, simply because they were seen entering a church on a Sunday, just out of curiosity. But the revival has changed that. Cuban churches today are full to overflowing and the house church movement has spread like wildfire – mostly due to inadequate church buildings and transportation problems in modern Cuba.

Totalitarian regimes reveal their fearfulness whenever popular movements of any kind develop in their country. This was the case with the fast-growing house church movement in Cuba in the early 90s. Even today, the government views the registered and in particular the unregistered Church in Cuba with deep suspicion, fearing they will develop into a political movement.

From the very beginning of these house church meeting points, the authorities were uncomfortable with them and inflicted every form of pressure from harassment to forced closure. Even days before the Pope's visit to Cuba in 1998, reports from some quarters tell of the police pressurising some house churches in Havana not to meet and telling their leaders to sign a form declaring they would hold no more meetings.

One house church which underwent considerable pressure from the authorities was located in central Cuba. On meeting days, the crowd coming to the church was so large (often numbering as many as 2,000 people), Pastor 'Pedro' would have to address the congregation in the streets from the top of his flat-roofed garage. The authorities siezed on this as a reason to arrest him in the spring of 1995. In just one day, he was tried, convicted and sentenced to nearly two years of hard labour imprisonment for 'disobedience' and 'illicit meetings'. This sentence was later commuted to 18 months.

'Pedro' had previously been ordered to close down his house church, but his bold response was, "The doors of my house are open. I will never close down a church that Jesus has opened."

For ten days, his wife and daughters were not allowed to visit him in prison. A major prayer campaign was launched around the world on his behalf. After serving half his prison sentence, he was allowed to return home on 2nd March 1996. He completed his sentence on probation.

After he was released, Pastor 'Pedro' told how God had supported him during his time in prison: "I am so thankful to God for all the prayers. I experienced the power of prayer. I received strength from God and was never ill. I had lots of opportunities to share the Gospel with my fellow inmates, who were amazed to see a Christian pastor inside the prison. They asked me if it was punishment from God, that I, as a pastor, should face imprisonment. I replied, 'No it is the love of God for you. He sent me here to share the love of Christ with you.'"

Another church leader who faced significant opposition was Dr. Eliezer Veguilla, a pastor's son. He studied medicine and became a doctor, but his passion was for youth evangelism. He served as president of the Baptist Youth World Alliance. Eliezer also formed a music group called Harp of David. The group toured Cuba, singing about the love of God. They wore T-shirts proclaiming 'Cuba Para Cristo' and popularised a song of the same name.

Eliezer was deeply involved in Bible and Christian material distribution throughout the island. He also travelled around showing the 'Jesus' film in many places. One night, he was due to show the film in a rural church when the police deliberately cut off the power. However, Eliezer had a small generator and since the church was the only building with power, the whole town turned up to watch the film!

On 6th January 1994, Eliezer organised a huge Christian

musical which was held at Havana's National Theatre. The authorities stood by in amazement as more than 3,000 people attended the concert – including the Minister of Culture and Religion!

Just weeks later, they arrested Eliezer as he was leaving the hospital where he worked. His 'crime' was being a Christian leader. The charges against him were of being a 'CIA agent'. Here's how he describes his prison experience:

"I was unjustly shut away in a prison dungeon. There were days in which, for over 16 hours at a time, they kept me in total darkness. I couldn't even see my own hands. I was the subject of intense interrogations, as well as physical and mental torture. I was switched back and forth between a boiling hot sauna and a freezing cold room.

One day, they showed me a ferocious-looking bear, with teeth and claws big enough to tear a man to pieces in a few seconds. A short time later, they threw me in a dark cell with what I thought was the same bear – but I soon realised this one's teeth and claws had been removed and it was chained. My torturers obviously expected me to panic and yell for mercy. However, I sat in a corner of the cell and to their astonishment, waited quietly for them to come and get me out.

On another occasion, they told me that I was going to be executed by a firing squad. As they 'prepared' me for it, I saw all the signs that it was going to take place that same day. It was one of the most difficult moments of my entire life. A few minutes earlier, I had heard screams of terror and then gunfire. Then they took me into the room where I was to 'die'. A trail of blood as though a corpse had just been dragged, ran from the blood-spattered wall to which I'd be tied, all the way to another exit door. The soldiers were already lined up, holding their rifles. As they stood in position, their leader asked me if I wanted to be blindfolded. Everything indicated that very soon I would be in the presence of the Lord.

'Don't cover my eyes. You are going to kill me without a reason and I would like to face my killers,' was all I could say at that point. 'God loves all of you! Jesus lives! Cuba Para Cristo!'

I heard the order, 'Fire!' Then came the click of triggers and the laughter of soldiers. The entire thing had been a mock execution. With the little strength left in me at that moment, I kept yelling, 'Cuba Para Cristo!' while my torturers continued to laugh.

All these events helped me to understand at a deeper level the true meaning of my faith. It was then that I understood our Lord was born with the purpose of coming to this world to be with us to have a beautiful ministry and to carry our sins in order to give us peace. He bore on his shoulders the result of our sins, which is suffering and death. Nothing that is done to us compares with what he suffered because of his love for us.

My wish for my beloved homeland is the same one for which all the Cuban believers have been fighting all along: 'Cuba Para Cristo'!"

After 47 days of interrogation and torture, Eliezer was released from the prison because the authorities couldn't find any evidence to convict him. They placed him under house arrest, and he and his family became the targets of constant surveillance and threats by officials. This forced them to leave the country on 15th September 1995. Today they serve the Lord in Miami. But their heart is with their fellow countrymen and their desire is still to see their country won for God.

You should have seen their faces!

He was travelling at twice the speed he should have on such roads. But then all taxi drivers seem to do this – especially in Cuba. Today, this driver had more on his mind than usual. He felt strangely warmed in his heart as his two foreign passengers told him about the special love they had for Jesus.

Helen spoke in English, while her companion, Elizabeth, translated into Spanish. Then Helen did something no passenger had ever done for him before. He automatically slowed down the speed of the taxi as she began to sing, "There is a Saviour…"

Something was really different about these girls. And Helen's singing was so sincere and moving. She really believed in this Jesus who died but lives. As Elizabeth told him about God's simple but profound plan of salvation for every person, the taxi driver couldn't hold back the tears. Stopping the taxi at the side of the road, he bowed his head and prayed the sinner's prayer.

And the angels in heaven rejoiced – again!

The angels have had much to rejoice about in Cuba these past ten years. 'Revival' is the word most Cuban pastors use to describe the tremendous Church growth in this period.

Though very limited in their outreach by Fidel Castro's attempts at containment for nearly 40 years, the Church has had a significant impact on Cuban society through the overflow of the Spirit from their lives. There are many hundreds of testimonies of conversions to Christ in Cuba after God's outpouring through signs and wonders. God's Spirit is at work in this country and his angels are kept rejoicing.

One of the best ways to bring encouragement to believers in Cuba is through a personal visit. Although restrictions on churches are more relaxed now than they have been, key leaders are still kept under close scrutiny by the government. They need to know that they are continually held in the thoughts and prayers of other believers around the world. Many Cubans live in poverty and lack the basic necessities of life. Hymn books and Christian teaching books are in desperately short supply. You could be the answer to a Cuban's prayer.

Over the past years, literally hundreds of Christians have known the tremendous experience of taking practical help and encouragement to Cuban believers. The most common remark on their return home is: "You should have seen their faces!" Here are some of their stories, in their own words:

"One morning, I was having my daily devotions before leaving for work. Somehow, I was reminded of the Suffering Church in Cuba, but that was all. The next morning during devotions, I strongly had the impression that God was telling me to go to Cuba. I called the Open Doors office and told the person who answered the phone of my desire to go. That marked the beginning of an adventure that I shall never forget.

The flight was late arriving at Havana airport, and it seemed to me as if flights from all over the world had arrived at the same time. The entrance hall was packed, but immigration went smoothly. Then came the luggage check. The lady customs officer lifted our bags onto the table.

'Tourist?' she asked. Without even looking in the bags, she waved us on to catch the hotel bus. We were so relieved. In our bags was a consignment of Bibles and Christian literature she would have confiscated had she discovered them!

After breakfast the next morning, we caught the bus, lugging our heavy loads of precious literature. We went into a hotel to phone for a cab, but the phone wasn't working. We asked different people for directions to a taxi stand, but it seemed that each new piece of information conflicted with the last.

It felt like we walked for miles and miles with our heavy load. It was hot, humid and dirty. I was already feeling physically weak and emotionally vulnerable from bouts of insomnia, which plagued me. I cried out, 'Lord, this is one of the most difficult things I've ever had to do in my life, and I haven't even begun it yet. You've got to help me!'

We finally found a taxi stand and then went to the church. Carlos, the pastor, a very friendly and loving man, led us all into a room and bolted the door. One by one, we then unloaded our Bibles and books. He was so appreciative of our gifts.

At the church, I met a 21-year-old Cuban Christian called Francisco. He was avidly studying English and between his skills and my Spanish dictionary, we managed to understand each other. Carlos and Francisco took us to a nearby cafe and intended to treat us to ice cream as a thank you, but we refused to let them pay for anything. They have so little in Cuba – and we have so much. When we finally finished queuing and sat down to eat, Carlos and Francisco spontaneously burst out in joyous thanksgiving to the Lord as if he had spread out a feast before them. This is one of the incidents which showed me how very much I take the Lord's abundant gifts to me for granted.

Even as we were eating, Francisco, in his limited English, quoted verses from the Bible to encourage us all. This really moved me to tears.

The next evening we attended a youth service at another church. We divided the remaining Bibles between us to take to the Christians there. When we reached Pastor Santos' house, the electricity had gone out and he was trying to light a kerosene lamp. We met his wife and other members of the family – again I was struck by how warm and friendly these people are. We unloaded the Bibles, relieved that this part of our mission had been successful. As we were emptying our bags, Pastor Santos remarked, 'The brothers and sisters from abroad are doing a wonderful work.'

We then went downstairs to where the church service was being held. The youth service had already begun. As we entered the room, I noticed that they had cymbals, a trombone, drums and a piano. The service was conducted entirely by the young people in the church. Even the sermon was preached by a member of the youth group.

I was thrilled to see the spontaneous praise that came from these people. We were then introduced to the church, and took turns in conveying a message to them. I had been so moved by the entire service that I was literally in tears by the time it was my turn to speak.

I sensed the warmth and love of the Christians, so I felt very free to be honest in giving my testimony. I started off by saying, 'I come from a family with many problems…' and concluded with the rest of my testimony.

Afterwards, we kept on praising God. While we did so, I felt someone's hands on my shoulders. It was Pastor Santos' wife, praying for me.

At the end of the service, people came up to us, saying, 'God bless you,' and indicating that they really appreciated our coming all that way to be with them. One lady said to me, 'I'll always have you in my heart,' placing her hand on her chest. They were very warm and friendly Christians.

God blessed us mightily through the graciousness of Pastor Santos and enabled us to accomplish our mission. He is a very bold and courageous man of God. After we had delivered the Bibles, I asked him, 'We're placing you at risk, aren't we?'

He answered with his hand on his heart, 'Risk? What risk? I took a risk when I accepted the Lord Jesus Christ as my Saviour and became a minister. And if they want to shoot me, so much the better. I'll go into glory sooner.' I am profoundly grateful to this very special man of God who has taught me so much by his life."

"She sat in her rocking chair, gently moving back and forth. In between praising and thanking God, she would stop every now and then to kiss the new Bible we had just given her. It is a moment indelibly planted in my heart. I love God's Word. But to watch the tears on this elderly woman's face as she hugged her new Bible close to her heart touched me deeply.

The elderly couple we were visiting went on to tell us how they had prayed for years that they would have their own copy of God's Word. But, they told us, Bibles in Cuba are in short supply. Little did they know how God was going to answer their prayers.

While we were trying to find a church where we were supposed to deliver our consignment of Bibles, we got completely lost. We prayed and felt that God was telling us to stop at a little house and ask directions back to the area we were looking for.

We knew we had to be terribly careful, or we could get the church leaders into big trouble. As we approached the front door, we asked God to guard our conversation, so that we would not create any suspicion. The old couple who opened the door asked us in immediately and were so friendly. Hand-made Scripture wall hangings were everywhere. It didn't take us long to find out they too were Christians, and we were able to share together like family.

Just before we left, with new directions to get to the church, we asked if they had a copy of the Bible. They said no, but they believed God would give them one someday. Thank God – today was the day!"

"One day I heard the Lord say, 'I want you to be a courier to Cuba for me.' I was overjoyed and so were my friends who agreed to go with me. As we began to read and research about Cuba, God showed us things that would be useful to take to those we would visit.

For example, four different Christian articles highlighted the need for women's underclothes. And so our women's prayer group got together and bought some clothes. Sounds like fun? It was! It was even more fun giving over one hundred garments to our Cuban sisters. They were so thrilled when they heard about the 50 women who had given the gifts for them.

Another example is the need for children's shoes. We found ten pairs of leather children's shoes in a sale – for the price of one pair! Matthew 6:30 kept coming to mind, *'If that is how God clothes the grass of the field, which is here today and tomorrow is thrown into the fire, will he not much more clothe you..!'*

One of the women preparing to go with us felt she should take some children's Bibles with her. As she prayed about what action to take, she saw an advertisement in a Christian magazine. It was offering children's Bible material for anyone going to Cuba! As she called the number given, she found herself talking to the author of the materials. Instead of one Bible and booklets, he sent her a full box of Bibles and materials for children!

Another friend loves street evangelism. She felt she should take a clown outfit and balloon kit with her. She learned how to make animals with the balloons. When she arrived in Cuba, she didn't get a chance to do any street evangelism herself, but she trained a young teenager how to make the balloon animals, and then gave him the clown outfit and balloon kit. He now uses this to evangelise!

As we entered Cuba, we didn't see anyone smiling. There was so much pain and hopelessness. During the first few days of our stay, the oppression was unbearable. Psalm 91:9,10 brought me so much comfort, *'If you make the Most High your dwelling – even the Lord, who is my refuge – then no harm will befall you, no disaster will come near your tent.'*

For security reasons, we were unable to leave our resort when scheduled. So we went on prayer walks around the resort and on the beaches. We were resolved if all we could do was pray, then pray we would. We then began to see waitresses smiling and little children playing.

The first Cuban Christian I met was a young medical student with a huge smile. What a contrast to the earlier hopelessness we had seen on the beaches. Eventually, we were able to stay in the homes of some believers. Another answered prayer! I couldn't speak a word of Spanish and none of my hosts understood English. My companion pulled out my Spanish dictionary and we used that to try and communicate. That alone drew us close.

I wanted to be with those who had truly stood firm in their faith. Again, God moved beyond what I could ask or imagine! One family member after another arrived to greet us. All were Christians, and all were pillars of the faith. In the back of my mind, I kept asking God, 'Father, where does this rich heritage come from?' Finally, I asked one family member who spoke English. He turned to 'Grandma' and said to her in Spanish, 'Grandma, show her your knees.' With that, Grandma showed me her two knees, calloused from years of prayer.

I learned that her husband had come to know the Lord only a few years before, after she had thrown herself at God's feet crying, 'Lord, I have seen you do miracle after miracle for my children and grandchildren. But Lord, I can't bear the thought that my husband still doesn't want to know you.' A little while later, her husband became a Christian. I cried as she told me the story.

We were asked not to do any street evangelism ourselves, as it might put the Christians at risk. But this didn't stop our friendship evangelism! One of Grandma's sons-in-law asked me to come to his house for tea. His niece was a medical student from another province. I assumed she was a Christian.

That night in church, I was asked to speak. This young medical student was there with her eyes intently studying my face. The next day I received a note saying that the young student wanted to speak with me. Grandma and her family were so excited, because this young girl had wanted to know nothing whatsoever about Christianity. She was committed to the Communist cause.

As I met up with her, I prayed desperately, 'Father, help. What message do you want me to give Maria?' Then I spoke, 'Maria, do you remember my saying last night how I wanted to know my Creator?' She nodded thoughtfully, 'Yes.' Then I asked, 'If you are a Communist, you probably don't believe in creation, do you?'

At that, the words came tumbling out. 'I used to laugh about Christianity,' she began, 'but when you were talking about God last night, he seemed so real. I don't know now. I'm so confused.'

After two meetings, she gave her life to Jesus. The first letter I received on returning home was from Maria: 'I keep reading my Bible. It's the most wonderful book in the world. I love my Lord so much!'

Maria's mother recommitted her life to the Lord and in her last letter, Maria wrote that her brother is now becoming interested in Christianity too.

On one of my morning walks, I saw a small group of middle-aged people in the street doing exercises. I thought to myself, 'That looks so refreshing!' I walked over and they invited me to join them. We had so much fun. Afterwards, one man in the group came over and hugged me and thanked me for joining them.

Grandma and her family had been watching us exercise from their kitchen window. They said they had been praying for me and crying at the same time, because this man was one of the staunchest Communist leaders in the area. They had never seen him express emotions of kindness or care. This to me was a ray of hope of good things to come.

We finally returned to the resort and on the last night, we held a worship service on the beach with our new friends. We heard one waiter ask the resort hostess why these tourists were bringing their Cuban friends to the eating areas where other Cubans are not allowed. The hostess replied, 'These tourists are Christians.'

I recently received a letter from the Cuban believers we met who shared that revival is everywhere in Cuba now. Years and years of pain and toil are now reaping a harvest. God is good!"

When Pastor Eusebio encouraged Christians to go to Cuba, he suggested they also take practical gifts such as a watch or calculator. One courier left a large bag of Spanish Bibles with a pastor and his wife in the central region of Cuba. He was thrilled to see their joy at the gift. But then he remembered his other special presents. From his bag, he pulled out a calculator and a ladies' watch. He was amazed to see the pastor and his wife start to cry.

When he was composed enough to speak, the pastor told him, "We have two children. Our son is at university – he's one of the few Christians they've allowed in. His mathematics professor warned the class two weeks ago that they must get hold of a calculator in order to continue the class. Next Monday is the deadline. We have prayed every day for money to buy a calculator…but no money came – just the calculator!"

"Our daughter is getting married soon and she has only one earthly desire… to have a watch."

God is the Master Encourager and provides for his children in unique and miraculous ways. It is no wonder Christian travellers returning from Cuba continue to say, "You should have seen their faces!"

Glimpses of God

A missionary to Latin America recently visited Cuba for the first time. He describes his impressions of the Church on the island:

God gives his people joy even in hard times: I talked with two Baptist pastors who had spent three years in prison and forced labour back in the 60s. Both have remained faithful in the Lord's service, and have a very significant ministry as pastors today. As I attended one of the church services, with 250 people worshipping there, I was struck by the joy of these believers, many of whom had travelled for several hours to get to the service.

In 1 Thessalonians 1:6, Paul writes to those early believers, saying, *"You became imitators of us and of the Lord; in spite of severe suffering, you welcomed the message with the joy given by the Holy Spirit."* Over and over again, I was welcomed as part of the family of God. I had never met these people before, but came to feel so much at home. It was to me a glimpse of what heaven one day will surely be.

Pastors and people pray seriously: James 5:17 tells us that Elijah prayed earnestly and that prayer was powerfully effective. One Cuban pastor told me how he and his wife spend from five to six o'clock each morning on their knees, praying for the lost in their city of 60,000 people. I was told later how calloused the knees of that pastor are. They left a thriving church to respond to the call of God and move to their present location. At first, they found only nine people attending on Sunday mornings. The church building was falling down and no money was available. Often, the pastor and his wife were the only two people who turned up for the Sunday evening service, but they saw it as a good opportunity to pray for the church.

Now, just over two years later, 100 people are attending the church, most of them new Christians! The roof still leaks, there is only one hymn book for every five people and many believers do not yet have a Bible.

The same pastor told how after Sunday School the week before, he and another believer had gone to visit a family where two people had recently been killed. As they told them about Jesus, the whole family was saved. Next, they went to call on a man who was in trouble and had the joy of leading him to faith as well. Surely they are seeing the results of many hours spent on their knees in prayer.

We were astounded by the level of commitment and courage we saw amongst the believers. One pastor told us of how three years ago his church began a series of special meetings which, as God miraculously worked, extended for 45 days. A church building which would normally accommodate 400 had close to 1,000 in attendance, and the street on both sides of their corner location filled with 3,000 more. But they encountered violent opposition; the church was vandalized and the pastor was called in by the authorities to stop the meetings. He refused, and finally things calmed down.

Just three months ago, that same pastor was again called in by the government. This time he was given an invitation to address the Fourth Party Congress that was being planned in just a few months. However, he refused. When I asked him why he declined the invitation, he said it would have confused his congregation. He was not prepared for any compromise, even thought this invitation would have enhanced his own prestige.

Another pastor we met was called in by the authorities the month before we arrived in Cuba. He was considered to be one of the key figures in the island's house church movement. The government was concerned, because they had learned of the rapid growth of the house churches under his leadership. In just three months, 50 house churches had been established, with a total attendance of 900 people every week.

The pastor told how on average 50 people were coming to

Christ in those house churches every week! When ordered to stop, he simply answered that he couldn't. He hadn't begun this work – God had, and neither he nor the authorities could stop what was happening, regardless of what they did to him. Finally, they released him.

Acts 2:47 says, *"The Lord added to their number daily those who were being saved."* I was reminded of this verse when a pastor in Havana told of how his church was open every day. They held public services almost every evening – in the church and in people's homes. This was in addition to prayer meetings which took place four mornings a week in the church.

In the evening services, he said that there was never a service without someone finding Christ. I talked with another pastor whose church we visited – and he told that that five people had become Christians in their evening service that Sunday.

We learned of four older women who made a three day trip to a town 50 kilometres away and led 14 people to Christ. They have now formed a house church. One university student caught the vision of what God could do through her and other Christians. After finishing her studies in early December, she returned to her home town, some 300 kilometres away. In two months, she led 15 people to Christ, again opening her home to them for regular meetings. We also learned of another couple who had travelled 200 kilometres – a three day round trip – to pick up a relative. But, on that trip, they led 44 people to Christ!

In Cuba, even today, it is supposedly illegal to gather more than seven people in someone's house without a permit. Nevertheless, this is taking place all over the island, as Christians come together to learn more of God. Some of these meetings are by no means small – we heard of one group of 60 people and another involving 80. One pastor told us, "There is an explosion of evangelism in Cuba today, which is beautiful to see."

Often, when God pours out his Spirit in a special way, there is a tremendous hunger for his Word amongst his people – and even amongst those who do not profess to be Christians. This is certainly true in Cuba. I saw people's eyes fill with tears as we brought them Bibles. One pastor's daughter clutched the illustrated children's Bible we gave her and pressed it to her chest.

We learned of a book auction that had been held in Havana just a few months previously. Bibles had been sold for the equivalent of anything from one to ten day's wages.

Jesus said in Matthew 16:18, *"I will build my church and the gates of Hades will not overcome it."* In spite of prison and forced labour camp sentences in the past, and many restrictions in the present, the church in Cuba is alive and well. A materialistic, godless philosophy is still taught in school to children as young as five years old. There is a serious shortage of Christian study books. And yet the Church is still growing. So often it seems to take hardship to motivate God's people to become serious about sharing what they believe. This is certainly the history of the Church over the centuries.

What is happening in Cuba today is in part due to the foundation laid by faithful missionaries many years ago. The seed was sown, the witness established and the work continues. But, there is a vital dimension that God, by his Spirit, has brought to the Church in Cuba, that is thrilling to see. And this Church needs to be helped by prayer and with material resources.

It is thrilling to hear of the many miracles God is doing on the island of Cuba. It is tremendously challenging to see the calloused knees of those faithful Christians who spend literally hours in prayer, begging God to move in the hearts of their fellow countrymen. And it is just as exciting to know that we can play a part in praying with them, sending materials such as Bible study books, and perhaps even going ourselves.

This is the day of Jesus Christ in Cuba

On 20th June, Cuba's Communist leader, Fidel Castro, stood amongst a crowd of over 100,000 singing, chanting and banner-waving Christians. The location was Havana's Revolution Square – normally the scene of Castro's lengthy annual political diatribes. For the first time in over 40 years, Cubans from around the island were given official permission to come together in vast crowds to an open-air public venue in order to worship God.

For once it was Castro's turn to listen. As he and other senior government leaders watched from front-row seats, they heard Bible readings, choirs singing and Christian messages proclaimed. Christians in the crowd were overwhelmed to be part of something they had hardly dared believe would ever happen. One Cuban pastor commented, "Twenty years ago I was put in prison for three days for reading Milton's 'Paradise Lost'. This event today is a miracle!"

The Havana celebration was the culmination of a month-long series of 18 Protestant celebrations across the island. And it was the fourth successive Sunday morning celebration to be televised nationwide. Castro himself authorised the Cuban Council of Churches to hold these public celebrations – never before has he given Protestants permission for such wide-scale meetings.

His action contrasts sharply with the persecution suffered by the Church during Castro's time in power. Many Christians feel that a new era of openness is coming to the island. One 80-year-old lady, who took part in the Havana celebration said, "I am so excited. I've been waiting for this day after 40 years of desert wanderings. This is the greatest time in which to live as a Christian in Cuba! Thank God for his blessing."

Others are more cautious. And with reason. Although the celebrations created the impression of religious freedom in Cuba, in reality there is still strict control of religions. The government approved the celebrations, but every detail was under their control

– even the sound systems had to be rented from the Communist Youth League who had to receive invitations to sit with the 'dignitaries'.

One group of about 300 Americans found out the hard way. They were told not to distribute Christian literature outside church buildings to people on the streets. Some disobeyed and handed out literature – the entire group was placed under 'hotel confinement' until they returned to America.

The good news is that the name of Jesus was lifted high across the island of Cuba. Now is the time to pray that the government would follow this through with more freedom. Cuba is "white unto harvest". The Cuban Christians are totally dedicated in their zeal to follow their Lord whatever the cost and to win more souls for eternity. Many have stated that they are waiting for doors to open, so that they can go as missionaries to other Latin American countries and proclaim the Gospel here. Let us join them in praying that they may see this vision fulfilled.

Chronology of opposition to the Church in Cuba since the 1960s

January 1959: Fidel Castro arrives in Havana, defeating dictator Fulgencio Batista. Many evangelicals embrace Castro's changes, among which he promised to respect religious freedom.

13 November 1960: Rev. Ernesto Vasseur, the pastor of the Methodist Church of El Vedado in Havana, is jailed. The cause of his incarceration was a sermon that, although it made no reference to the revolution or its leaders, was considered anti-revolutionary. He is released two days later, after being threatened.

April 1961: Castro declares the permanent socialist character of the revolution.

1961: A massive exodus of Cubans, among them many pastors and Christians, flee to the USA. It is estimated that during this period, about 90 per cent of the island's Methodist pastors and 70 per cent of the Baptist pastors are amongst those leaving.

All Christian radio and television programmes are banned.

Religious schools become the exclusive property of the state.

1962: The Bible Society and all Christian bookshops are closed. All supplies of Bibles and materials are restricted to what each individual church may be able to obtain through the help of Christians abroad.

Rev. Domingo Fernandez, a Baptist pastor, and host of a well-known Christian radio programme, is forced to leave the country after receiving a number of death threats.

Rev. Bernardo Amor is imprisoned in the town of Colorado, while trying to stop his church being closed.

October 1962: Two churches in Sancti Spiritus are closed. Between this date and 13 March 1963, more than 60 rural churches are closed.

13 March 1963: The Theological Seminary of the Assemblies of God is permanently shut down.

September 1963: Deacon Jose Cano of the Pentecostal Evangelical Church of Tunas, is murdered for handing out tracts. After detaining him, the authorities send him to buy something. As he walks away, he is riddled with bullets. Soldiers claim he is trying to escape.

1963: In the province of Oriente, more than 45 churches of different denominations are shut down. Many rural churches throughout the island are mysteriously burnt.

A pastor from Los Pinos Nuevos Church in Placetas is brutally beaten and is hospitalised for two months. After leaving the hospital, he is asked the same question he was asked before the beating: "Will you stop preaching?" His reply is clear: "No."

1963-1968: Rev. Carlos Anderson, pastor and member of the Executive Committee of the Assemblies of God, is jailed several times in different cities.

1965: The three main leaders of the Gideon Evangelical Association vanish without a trace near Limonar. It is presumed that they were executed.

8 April 1965: 53 Baptist pastors and missionaries are sentenced from two to 30 years' imprisonment, accused of 'anti-revolutionary activities'.

November 1965: Pastor Ricardo Peña is imprisoned, along with the entire congregation of the Assemblies of God Church Primer Paso, in the province of Havana.

1965-1967: Hundreds of Christian young people are sent to labour camps along with other 'anti-social elements'. These camps are later shut down due to international pressure.

13 March 1978: Four pastors from the Assemblies of God; Adimael Rodriguez, Francisco Quintero, Hector Hunter and Eusebio Perez, are imprisoned for three days and forced to undergo intense interrogations.

February to October 1980: Assemblies of God pastor, Orson Vila, is sentenced to four months in prison for 'illegal healing' while he conducted an evangelistic crusade in the city of Moa. Rev. Daniel Hernandez, the pastor of the Baptist church where the crusade took place, is given three months in prison.

November 1982: Pastor Onelio Gonzalez's home in Nueva Gerona, is raided by the authorities. They find the book *Vanya*, which tells the story of the death of a young Christian man recruited by the Soviet army, along with some notes written by the pastor's son. Authorities threaten to sentence Rev. Gonzalez and send his son to a rehabilitation camp, unless his preaching credentials are revoked. In December 1986, Rev. Gonzalez is forced to leave Cuba.

14 May 1983: The pastor of the Buenas Nuevas Church, Jesus Exposito, is imprisoned for eight and a half months without trial and subjected to intense interrogation. He is later sentenced to two and a half years in prison for being the son of Pastor Gilberto Exposito, who had been sentenced to five years.

25 December 1986: Assemblies of God pastor in Havana, Rev. Hugo Vidal, is subjected to two days of intense interrogation after showing a Christian video. His credentials are revoked and he is eventually forced to leave the country in 1990.

13 February 1989: Abel Sanchez and Auspicio Rodriguez, pastors from the Assemblies of God church in Contramaestre, are imprisoned along with 11 other members of their church, including two 65-year-old men.

September 1993: Lay pastor Miguel Angel Leon from the Baptist church in San Fernando de Camarones, is imprisoned with another member of his church, Jose Brito. Although none of the accusations could be proved at their June 1994 trial, they each receive a five-year prison sentence.

1994: A crowd surrounds the Methodist Church of Manzanillo, yelling Communist slogans and demanding that Pastor Juan Carlos Gonzalez be turned over to them, dead or alive. Through the intervention of Bishop Rinardo, he is able to flee to Havana.

The pastor from one of the Assemblies of God churches in Camaguey, Rev. Benjamín de Quezada, is savagely clubbed.

January 1994: For several months, pastors and church leaders are continually subjected to thorough interrogations regarding their Christian activities, especially if they are related to a house church.

24 January 1994: State security agents detain Dr. Eliezer Veguilla, along with other Christian leaders and pastors, and accuse them of being CIA agents. After 47 days of severe interrogation, Dr. Veguilla is released, but placed under house arrest.

April 1995: The leader of a Christian mission is ordered to close down his house church. When he refuses, he is brutally beaten by a police chief and detained. A pastor going to the police station to intercede for him is also detained. They are released on bail 12 hours later.

24 May 1995: State security agents arrive at the house of Pastor Orson Vila in the province of Camaguey, where a 1,500 strong house church meets. He is detained and sentenced to 23 months in prison.

June 1995: Several pastors from around the island receive a direct notification from the Ministry of Justice ordering the permanent shut down of house churches. The pastors and owners of the houses where the churches meet are threatened with fines and detention if they fail to comply.

16 December 1995: A seminary and other facilities belonging to the Buenas Nuevas Pentecostal Church in Cienfuentes are confiscated by the Ministry of Agriculture.

January 1996: Government authorities in the city of Colon, threaten Pastor Juan Carlos Rojas for refusing to cancel all his church weekend activities so that his church members can do 'volunteer work' for the state.

The authorities inform Pastor Alejandro Nieto of the Evangelical League of Cuba church in Havana that he is not allowed to buy paper, stencils, toner and other materials for reproduction work at his church. He is also not authorised any construction materials for repairs or additions to church facilities.

April 1996: Several pastors request prayer support, saying they are constantly called in by state security; threatened, interrogated and placed under strict surveillance.

A church in Tunas is stoned on several occasions. Every time there is a church service, loudspeakers playing secular music are placed in front of the church.

Open Doors International Vision Statement

We believe that all doors are open and that God enables his body to go into all the world and preach the Gospel. We therefore define our ministry as follows:

- To strengthen the body of Christ under restriction or persecution by providing and delivering Bibles, materials, training and other helps, and encouraging it to become involved in world evangelism.

- To train and encourage the body of Christ in threatened or unstable areas, to prepare believers to face persecution and suffering, and to equip them to maintain a witness to the Gospel of Christ.

- To motivate, mobilise, and educate the Church in the free world to identify with and become more involved in assisting the Suffering Church, believing that when *"one members suffers, all the members suffer with it"* (1 Corinthians 12:26 NKJV).

How you and your church can make a difference

Prayer – the believers in persecuted lands live in a fierce spiritual battlefield. They need focused, intercessory prayer. Open Doors prayer magazines and newsletters provide you with daily prayer items to enable you to pray for these brothers and sisters and stand beside them in their struggle.

Bible Couriers – for decades, Open Doors has been helping believers carry Bibles and Bible study aids into the areas of greatest persecution. God uses ordinary people to take his Word to people living where faith costs the most. You can be one of them.

Adult and Children's Bibles – many persecuted believers have been beaten and imprisoned for their faith, yet don't have a Bible of their own. The young people in persecuted lands are special targets for false teaching and government control. Leaders know they must have control of the minds of the youth if they are to stop the spread of Christianity. Open Doors is providing the Church with special adult and children's Bibles that present the truth through words and pictures. Your generous gifts make this possible.

Leadership Training for Church Growth and Evangelism – most church leaders in persecuted lands have never had any formal training. Bible Schools either don't exist or have been destroyed. Open Doors works to fill this vacuum in these lands with Bible-based training tailored to the needs and culture of each area.

Your faith can equip and encourage the future leaders of our fellow believers who suffer for their faith.

For more information, write to:

Open Doors
PO Box 53
Seaforth
NSW 2092
AUSTRALIA

Missao Portas Abertas
CP 45371
Vila Mariana
CEP 04010-970
São Paulo
BRAZIL

Open Doors
PO Box 597
Streetsville, ONT
L5M 2C1
CANADA

Portes Ouvertes
BP 141
67833 TANNERIES
Cédex
FRANCE

Porte Aperte
CP 45
37063 Isola della Scala
Verona
ITALY

Open Doors
Hyerim Presbyterian
  Church
Street No 403
Sungne 3-dong
Kangdong-gu #134-033
Seoul
KOREA

Open Doors
PO Box 47
3850 AA Ermelo
THE NETHERLANDS

Open Doors
PO Box 27-630
Mt Roskill
Auckland 1030
NEW ZEALAND

Åpne Dorer
PO Box 4698 Grim
4673 Kristiansand
NORWAY

Open Doors
PO Box 1573-1155
QCCPO Main
1100 Quezon City
PHILIPPINES

Open Doors
1 Sophia Road
#06-11 Peace Centre
SINGAPORE 228149

Open Doors
Box 990099
Kibler Park 2053
Johannesburg
SOUTH AFRICA

Portes Ouvertes
Case Postale 267
CH-1008 Prilly
Lausanne
SWITZERLAND

Open Doors
PO Box 6
Witney
Oxon OX8 7SP
UNITED KINGDOM

Open Doors
PO Box 27001
Santa Ana
CA 92799
USA

You can visit the Open Doors website on www.od.org